Published in 2016 by
Doolallytap
50 Gloucester Road
Cheltenham
GL51 8PA
Email: info@doolallytap.com
www.drawntothesea.com
www.doolallytap.com

ISBN 978-1530325276

Design: Paul R. White, Sabrina Impieri

For
Nina, Jack and Thomas

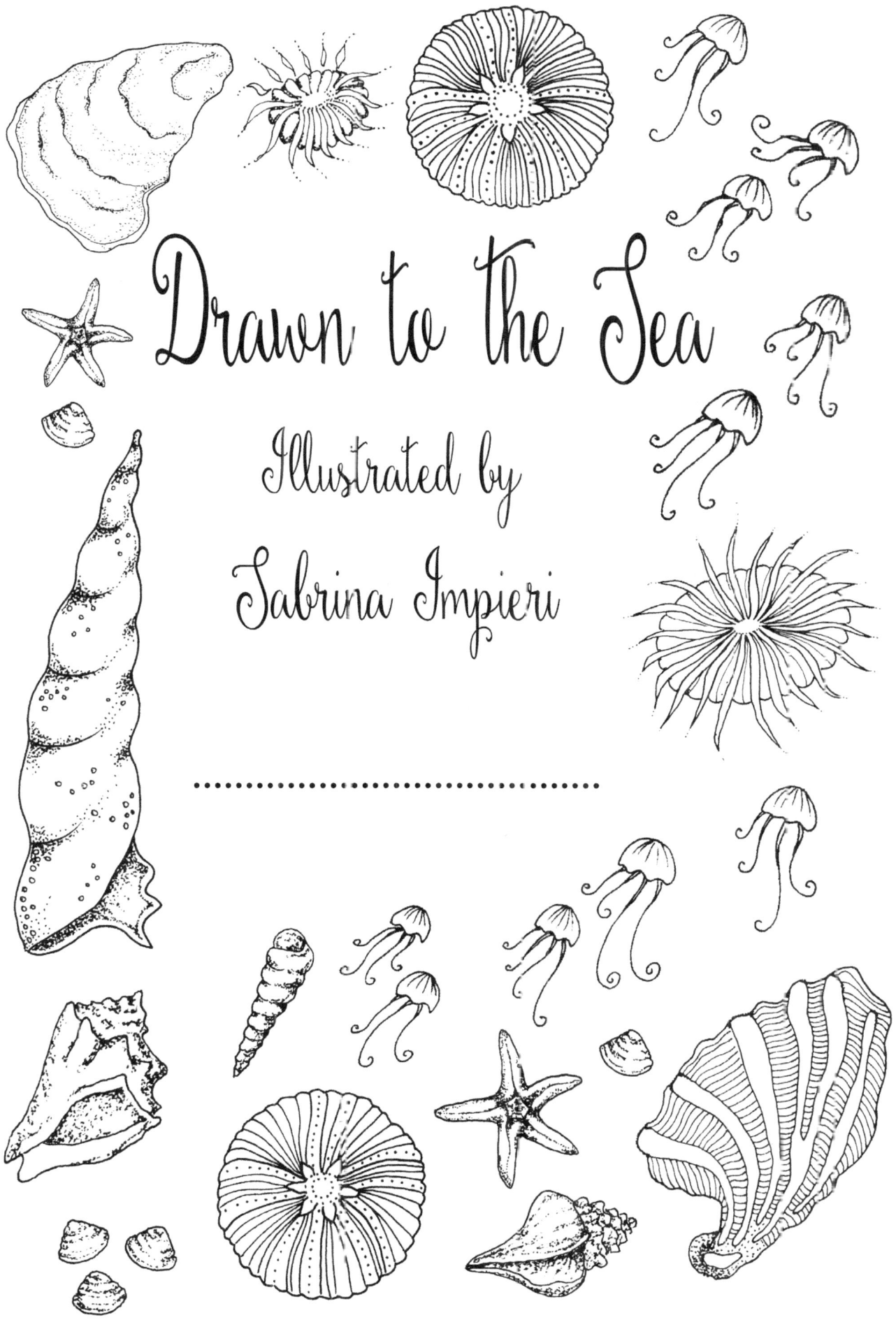

Drawn to the Sea

Illustrated by

Sabrina Impieri

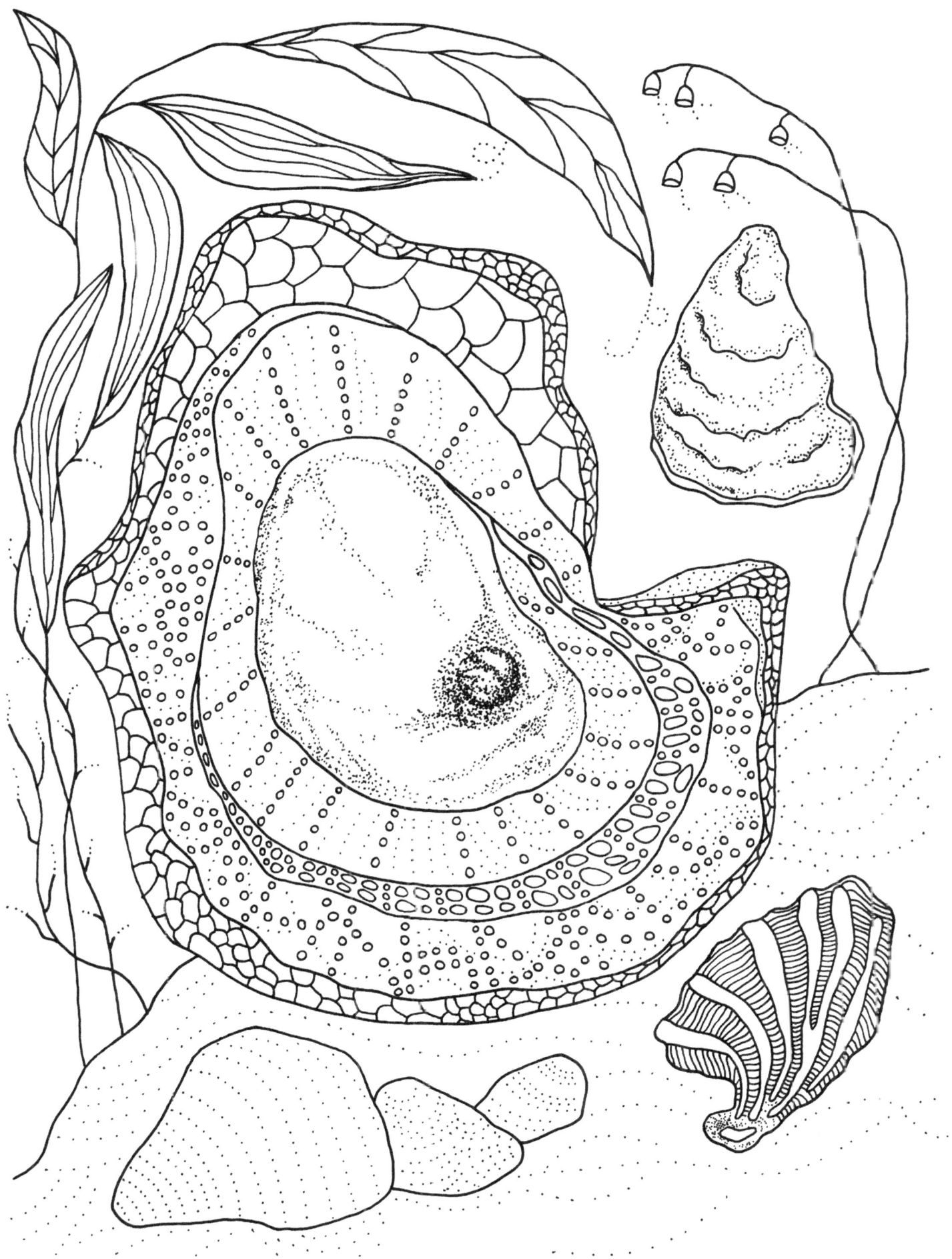

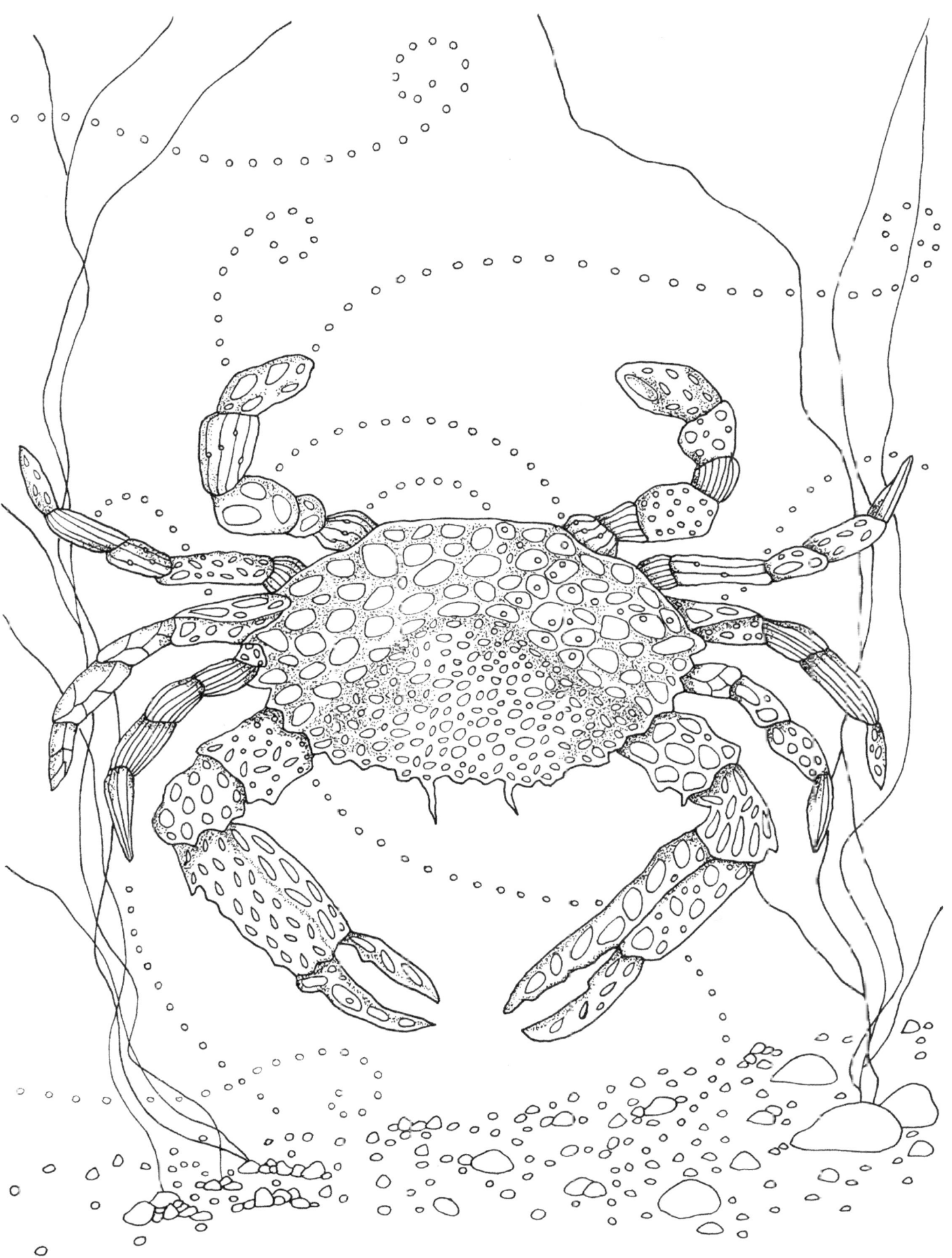

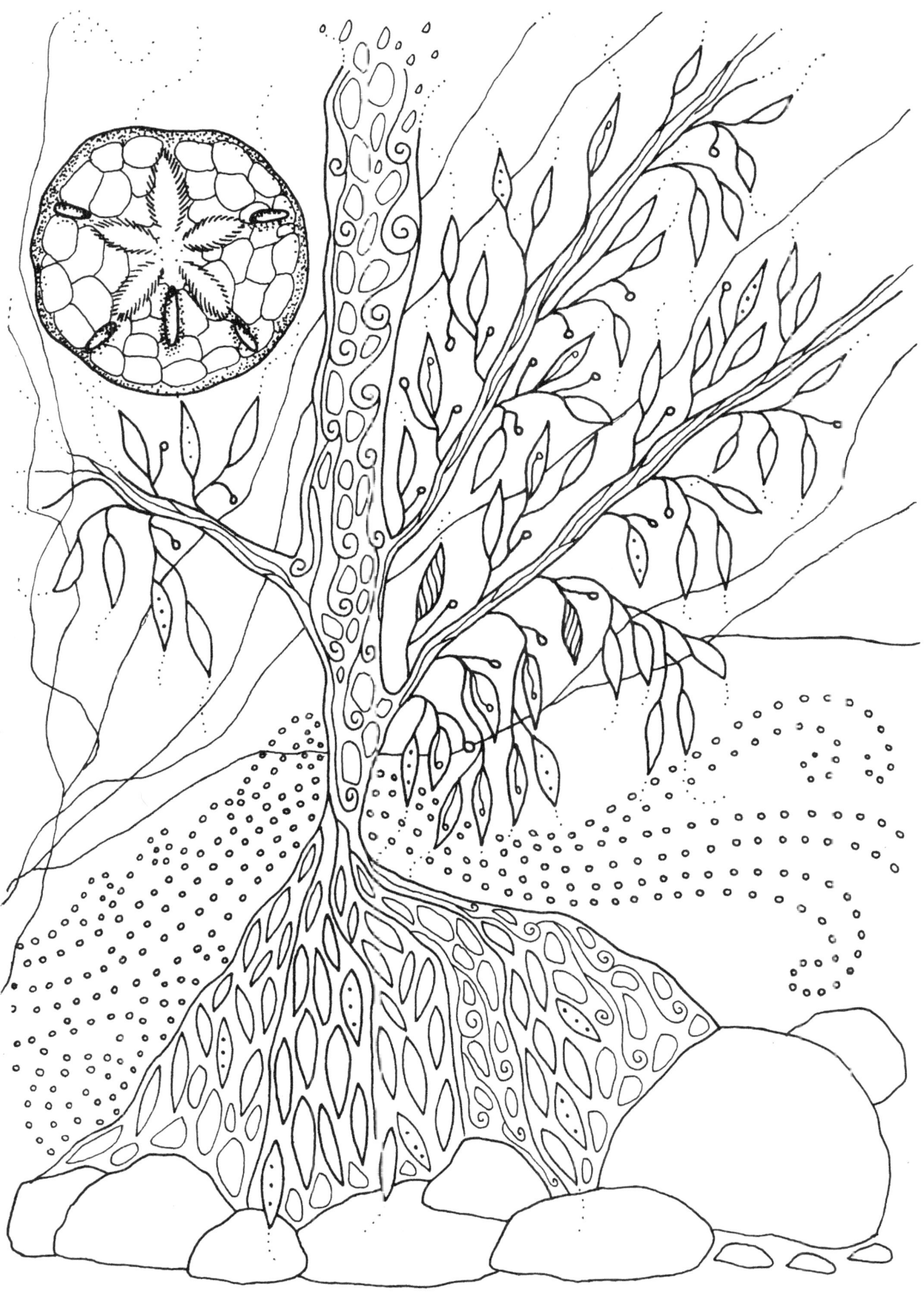

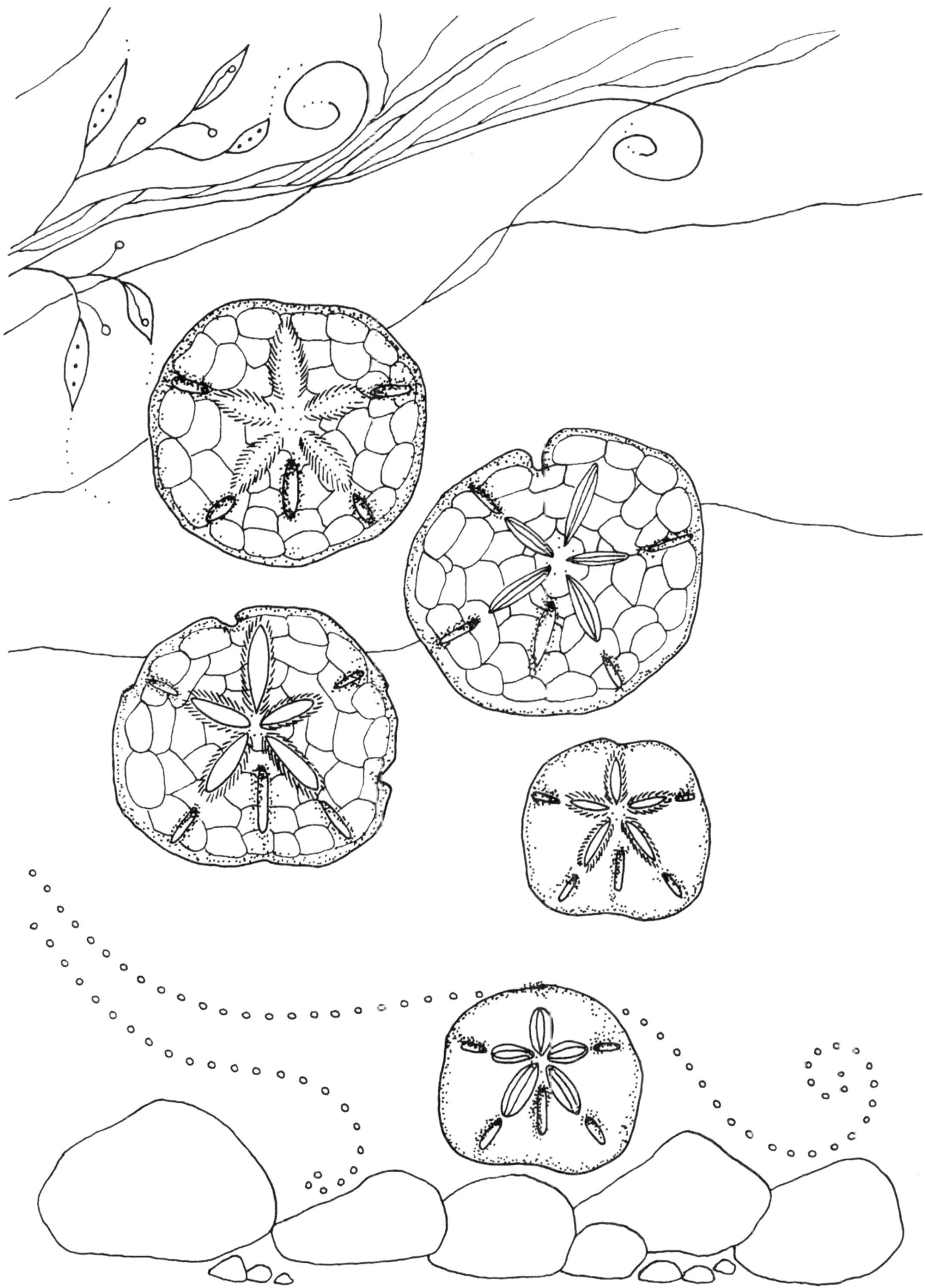

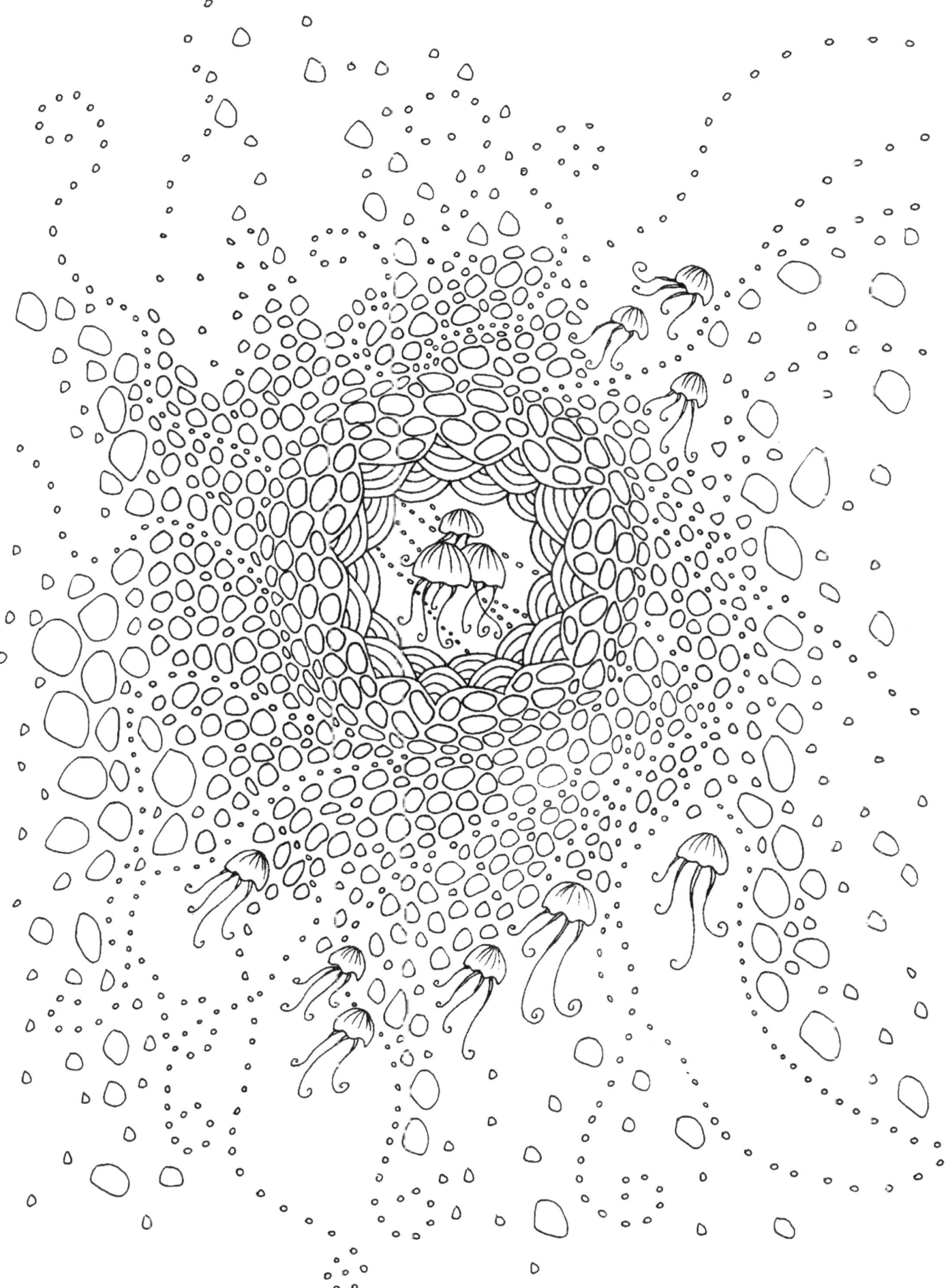

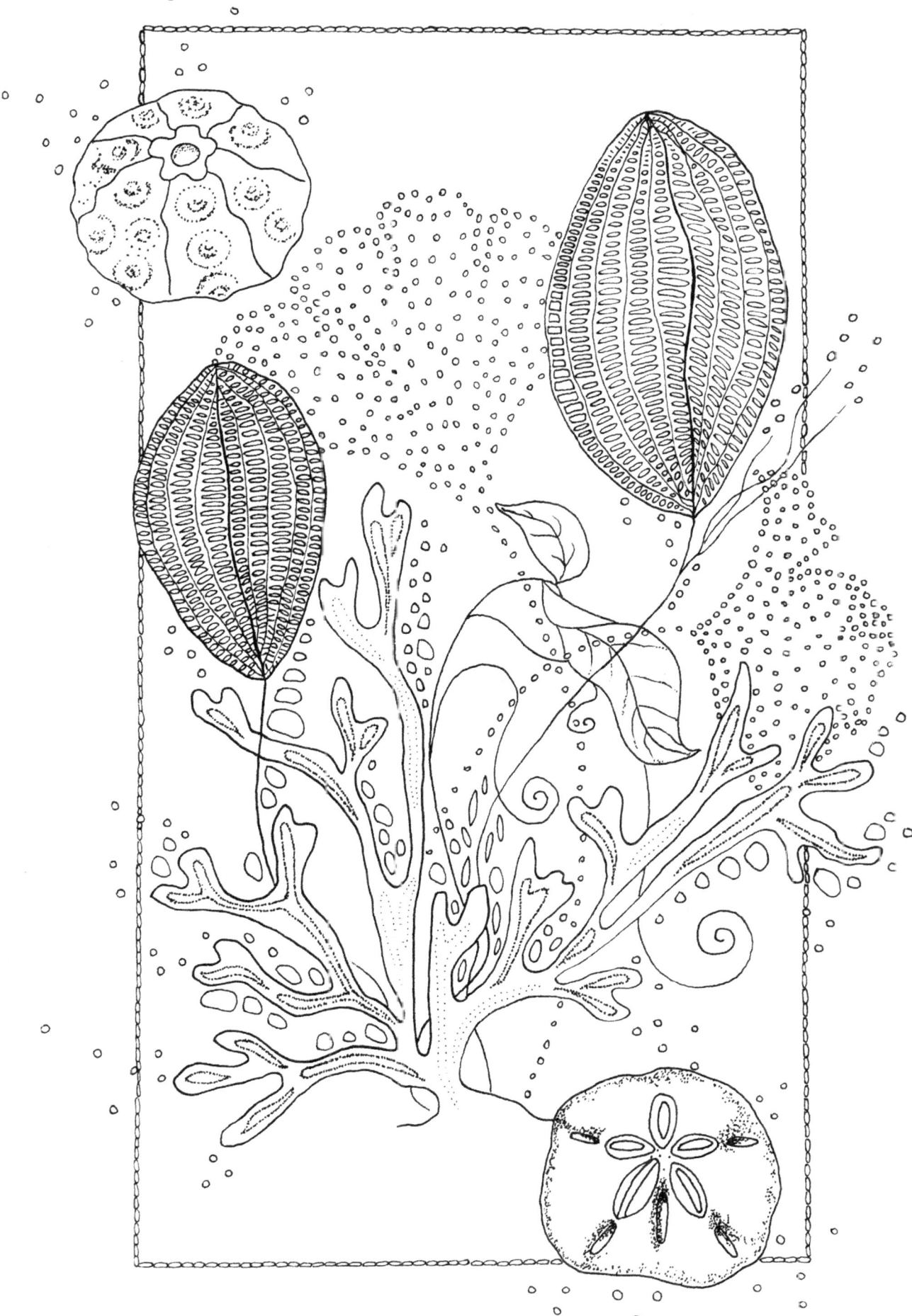

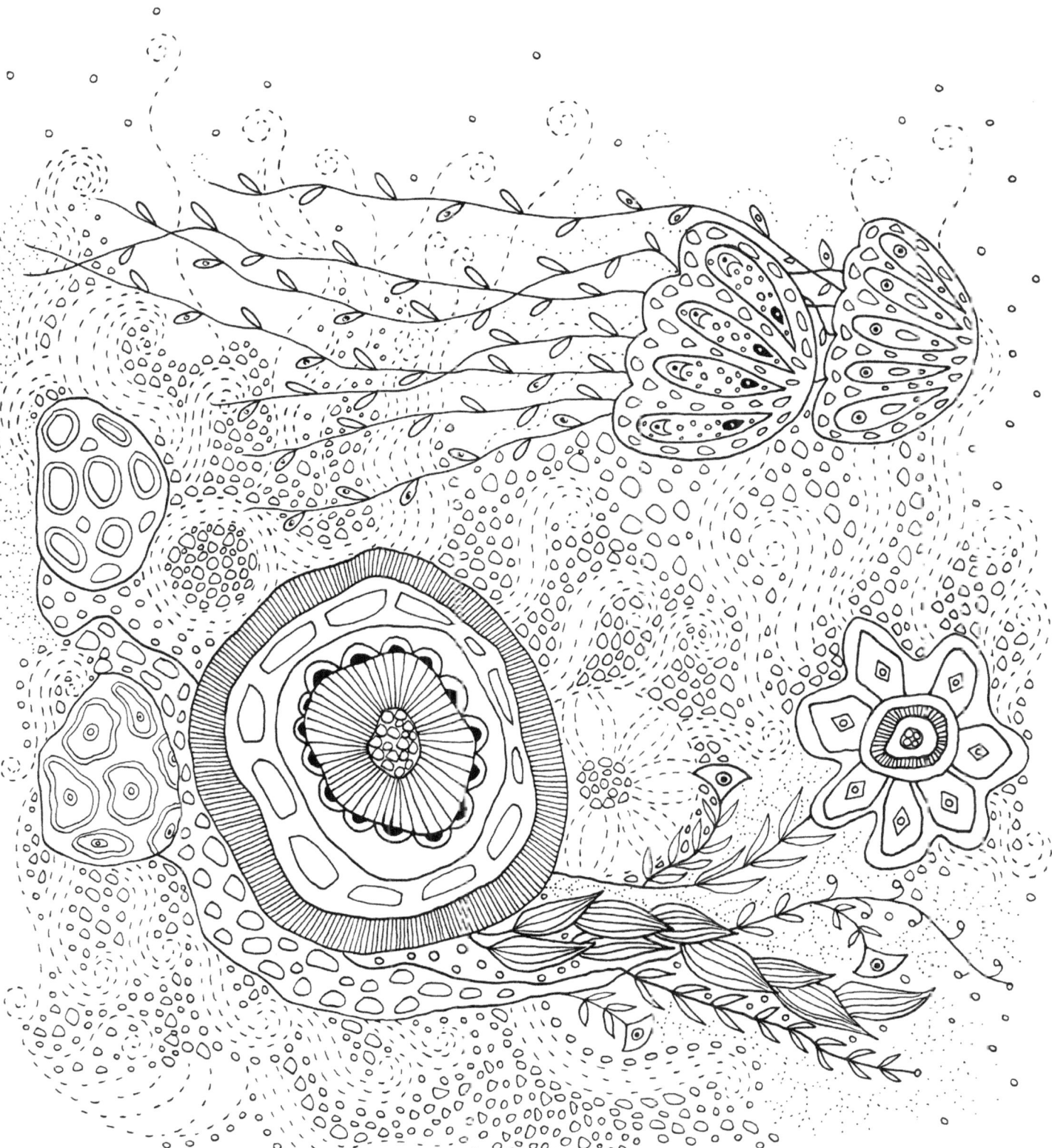

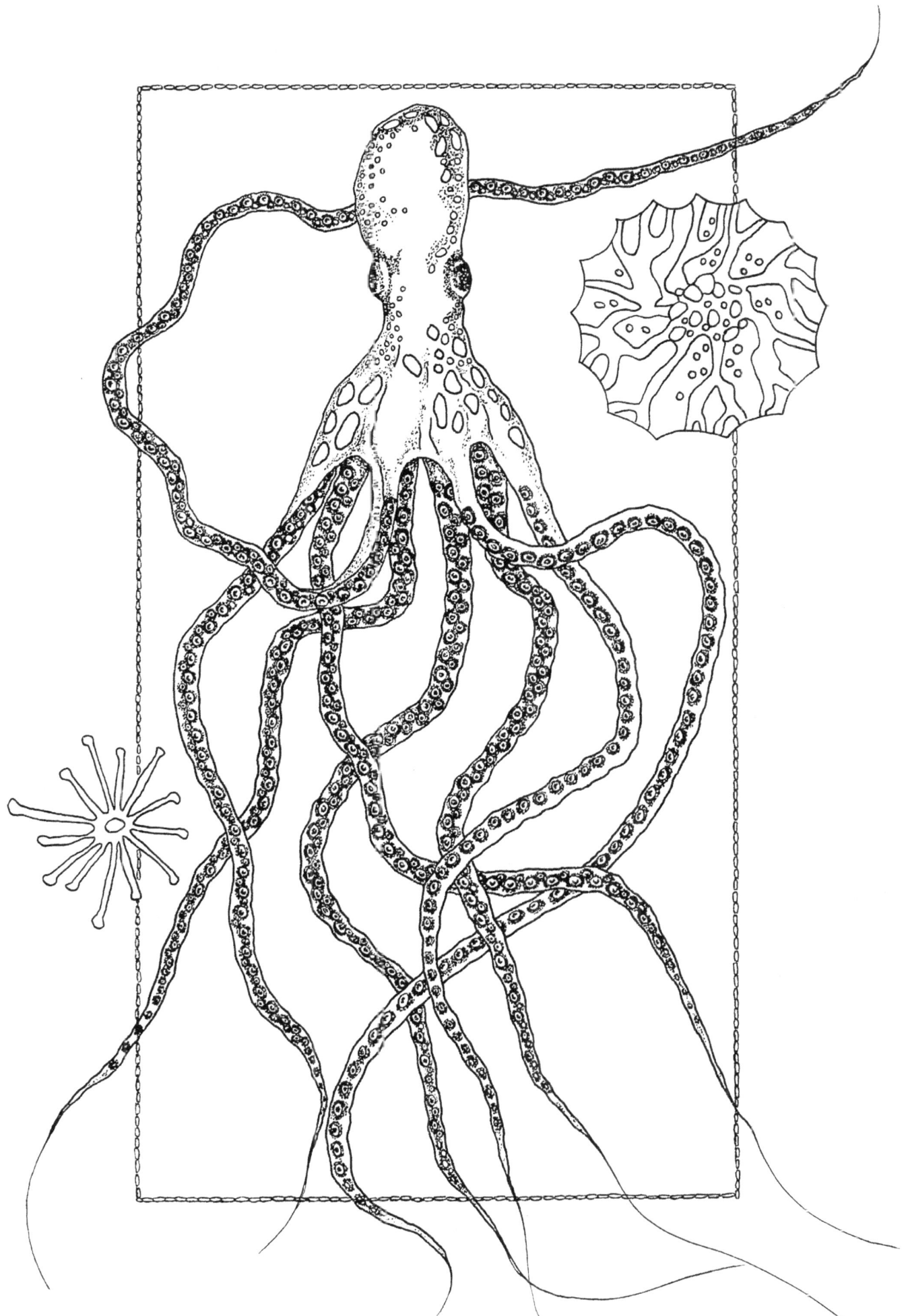

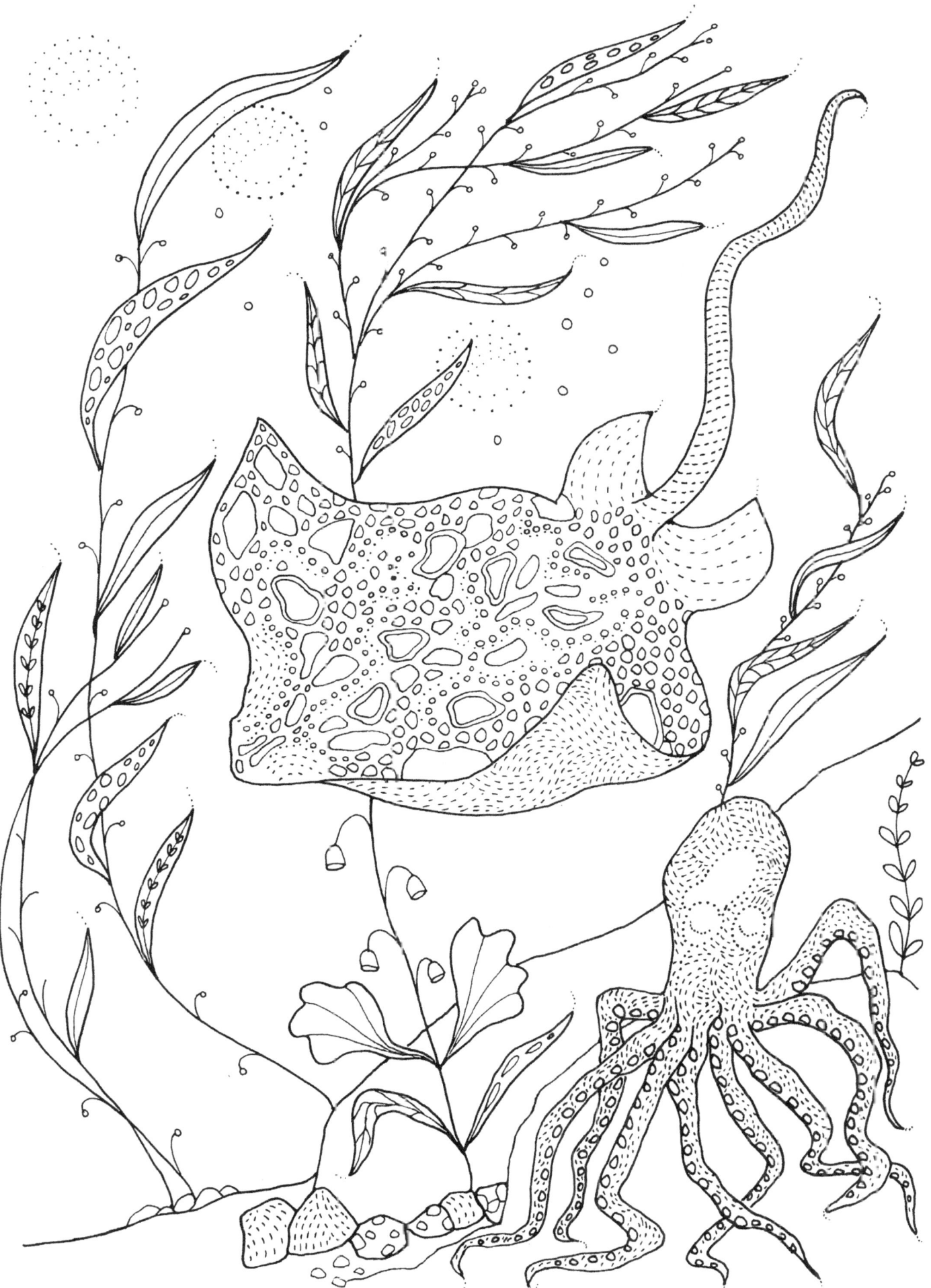

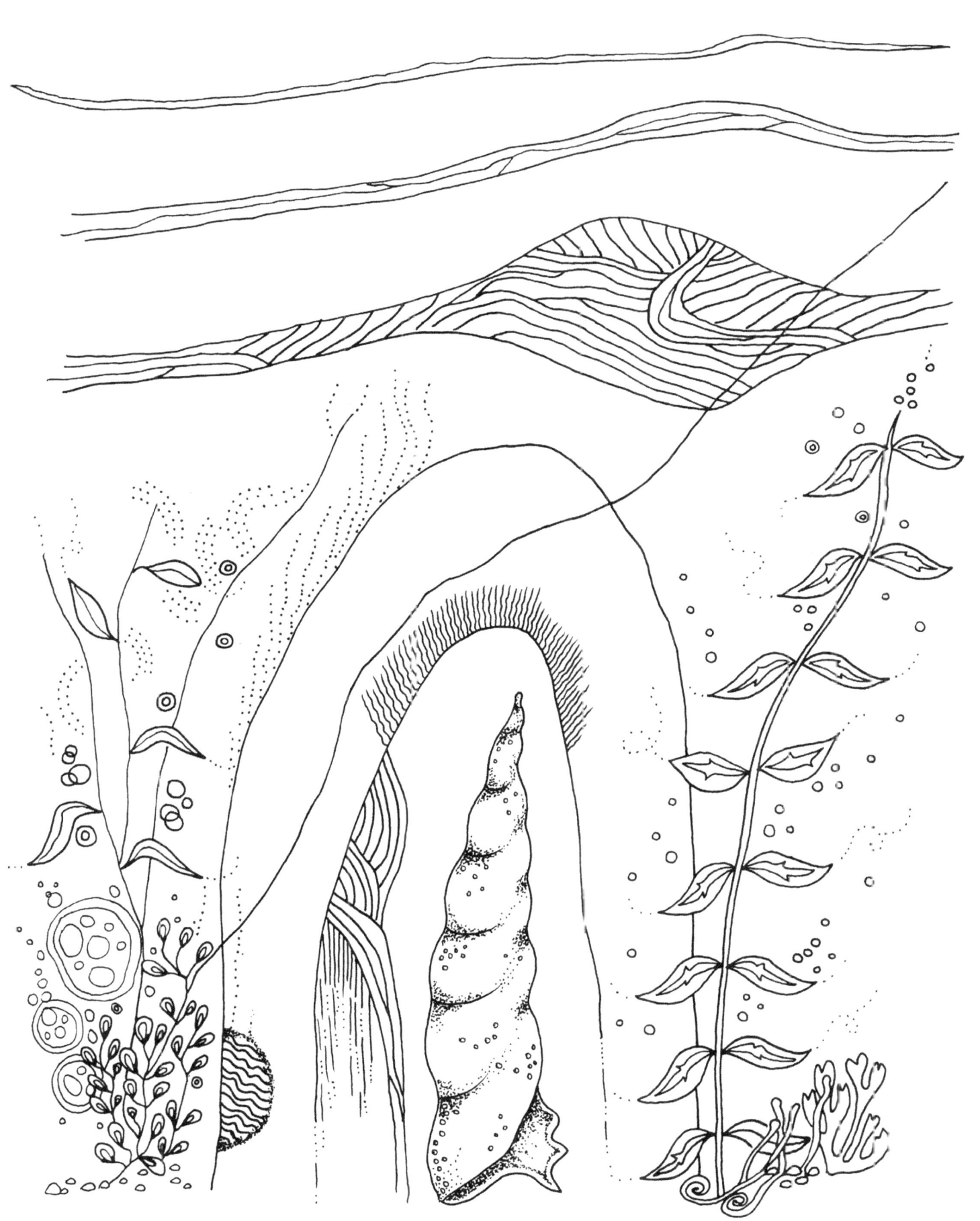

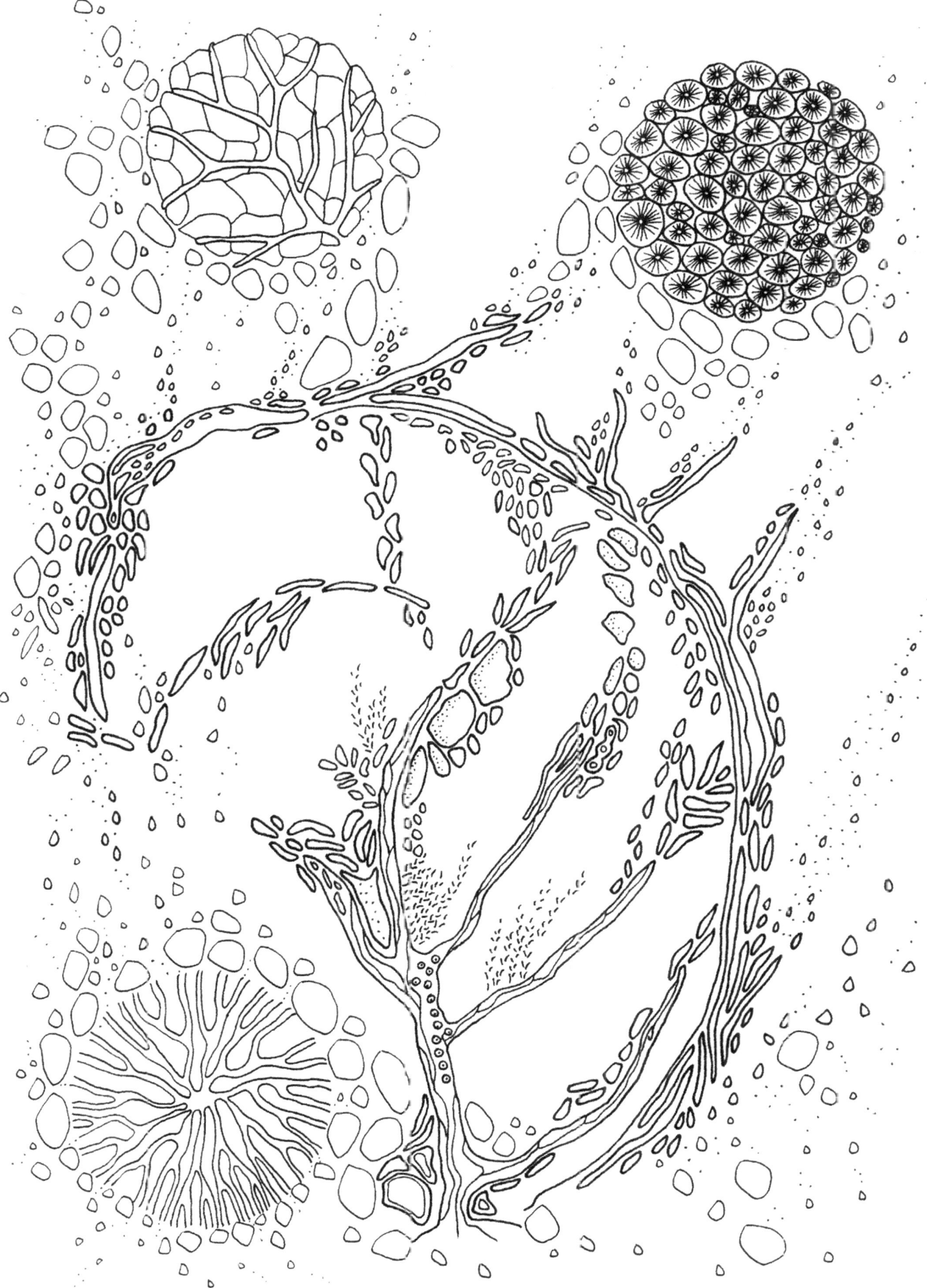

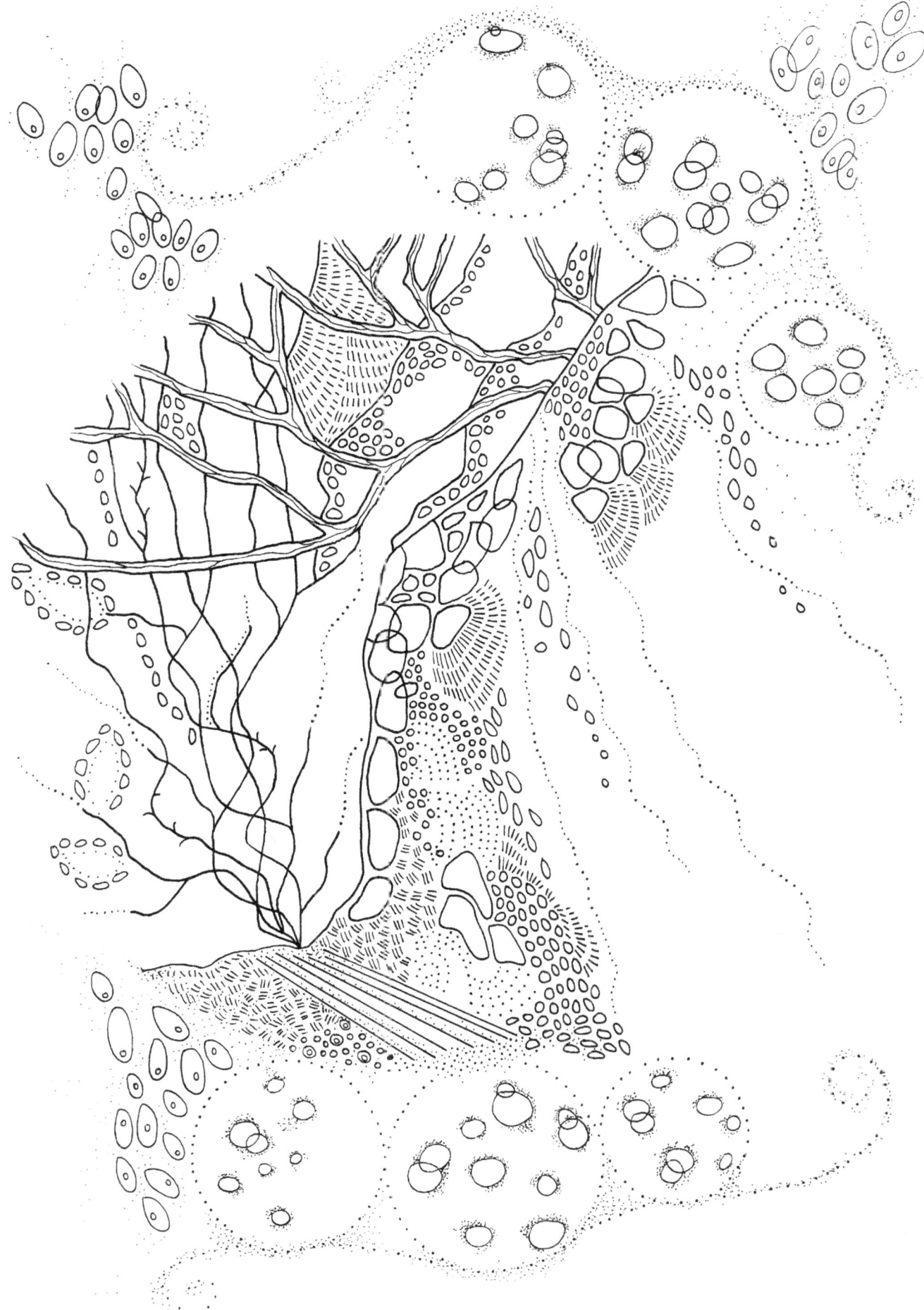

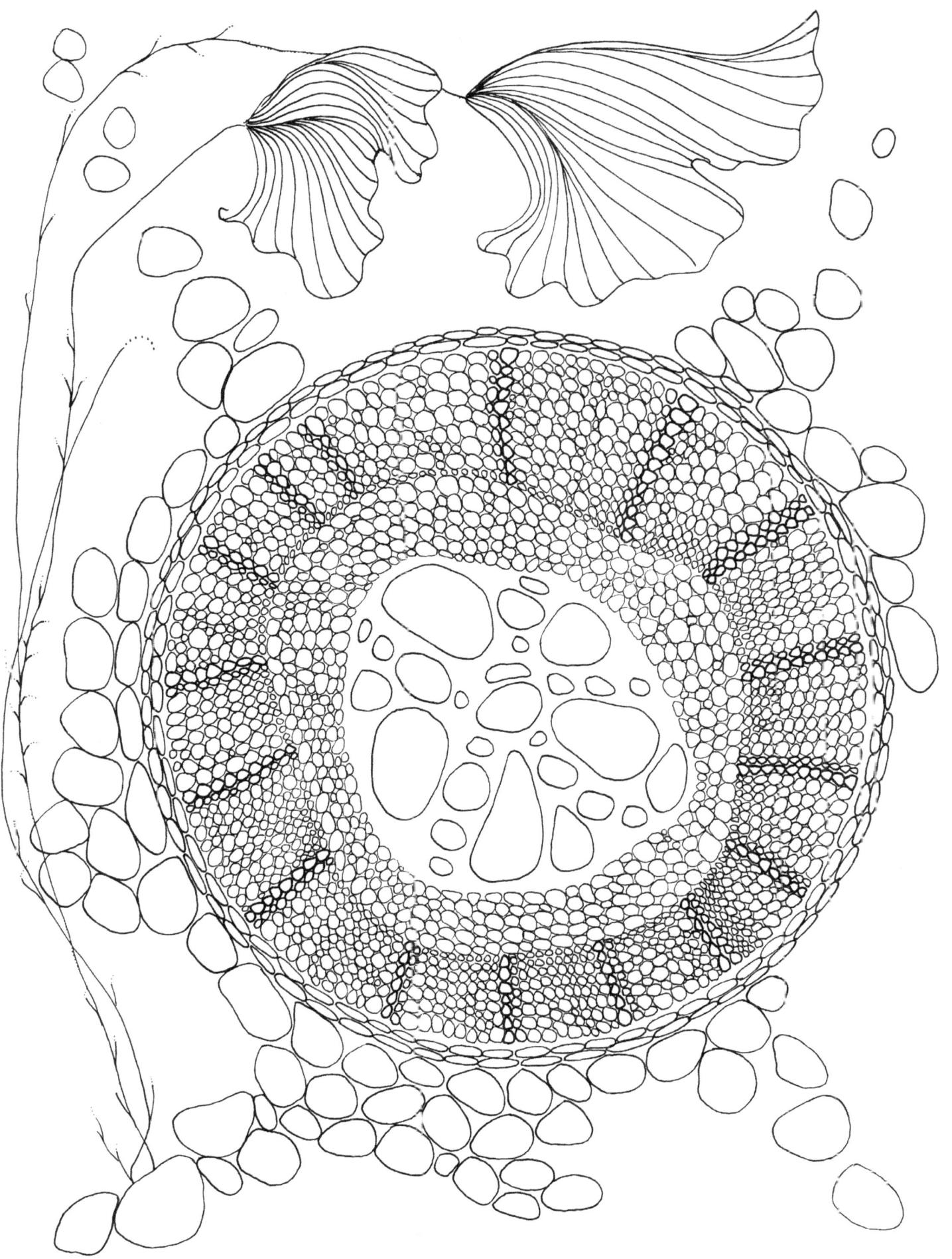

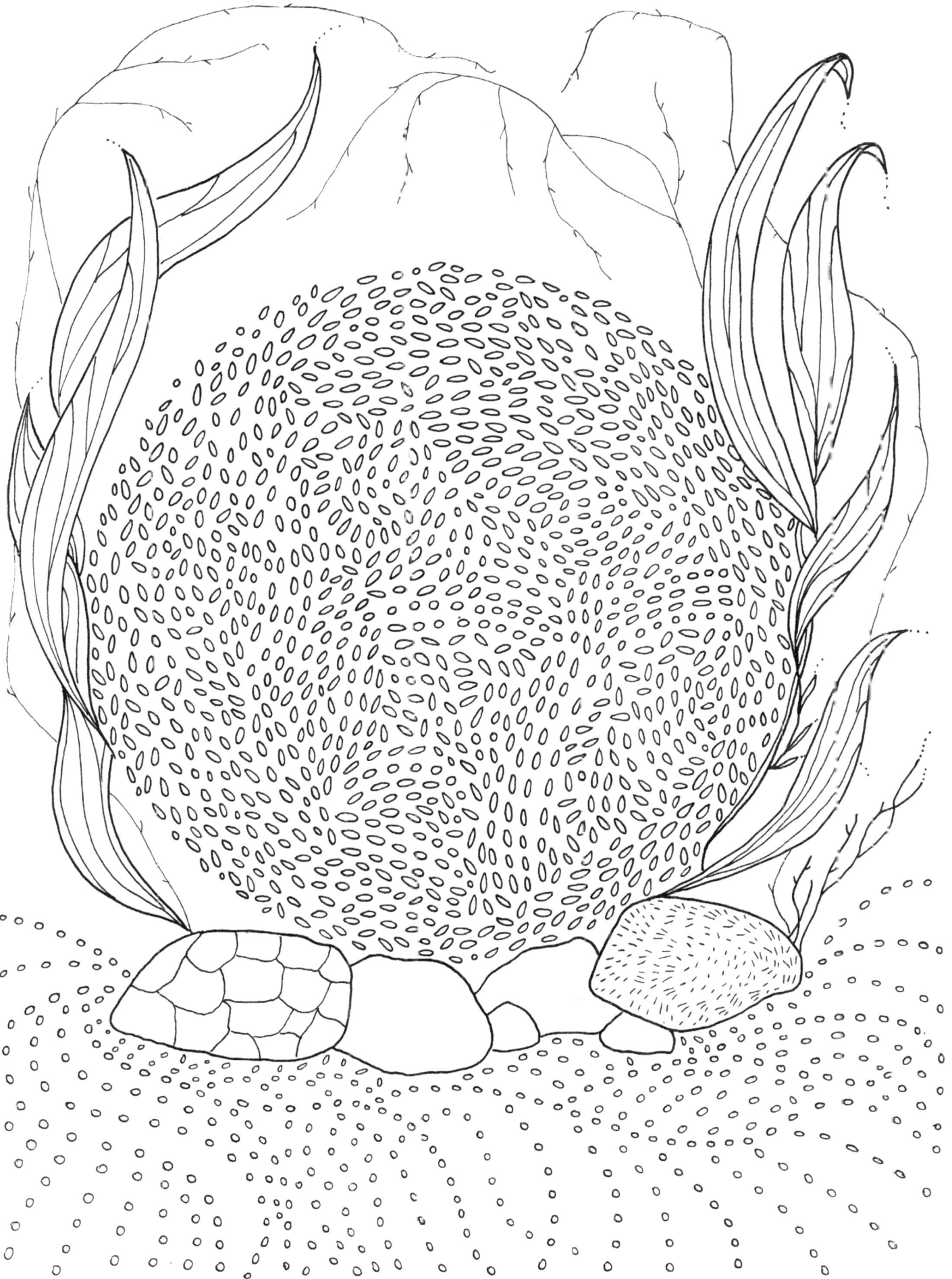

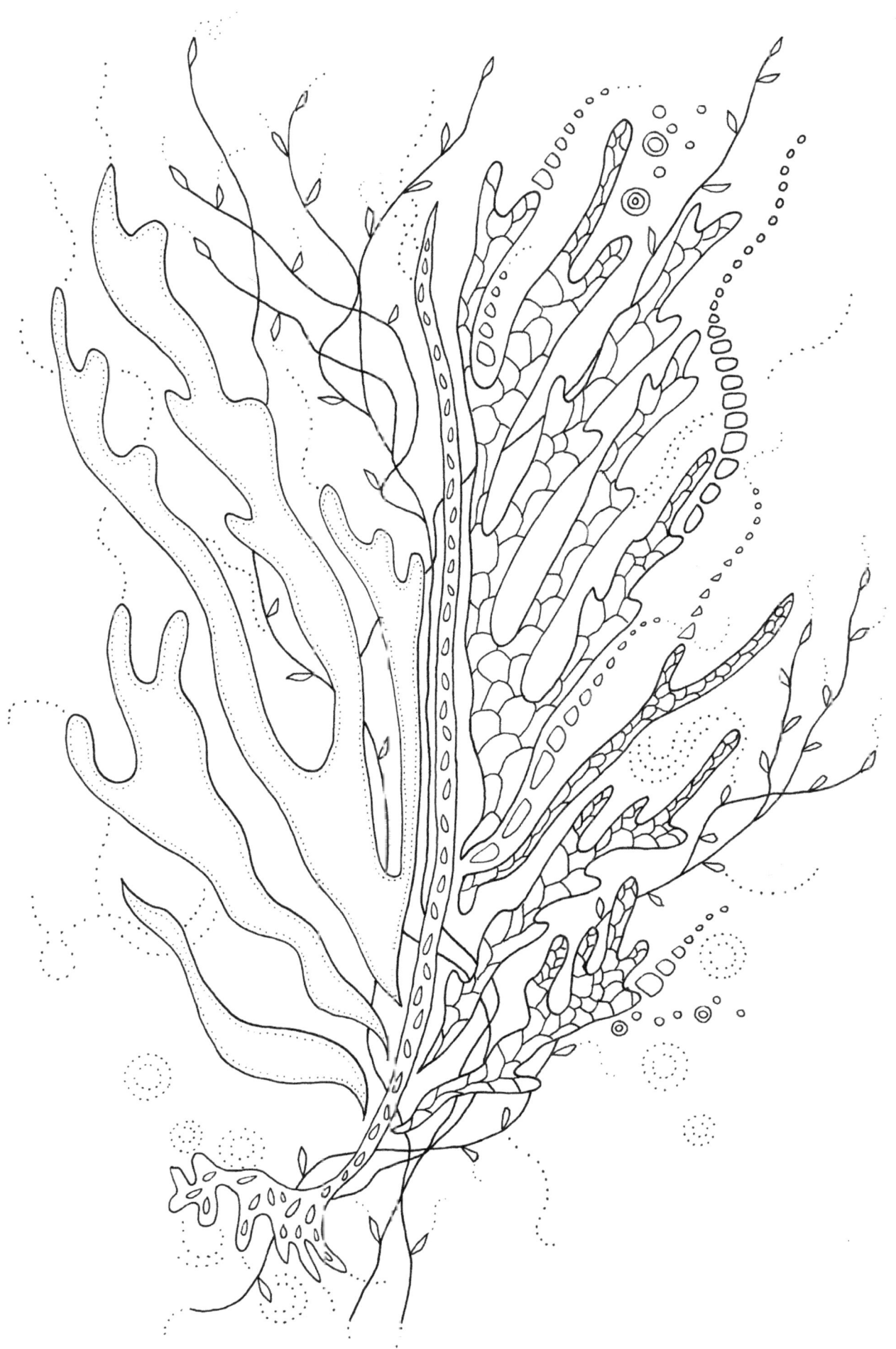

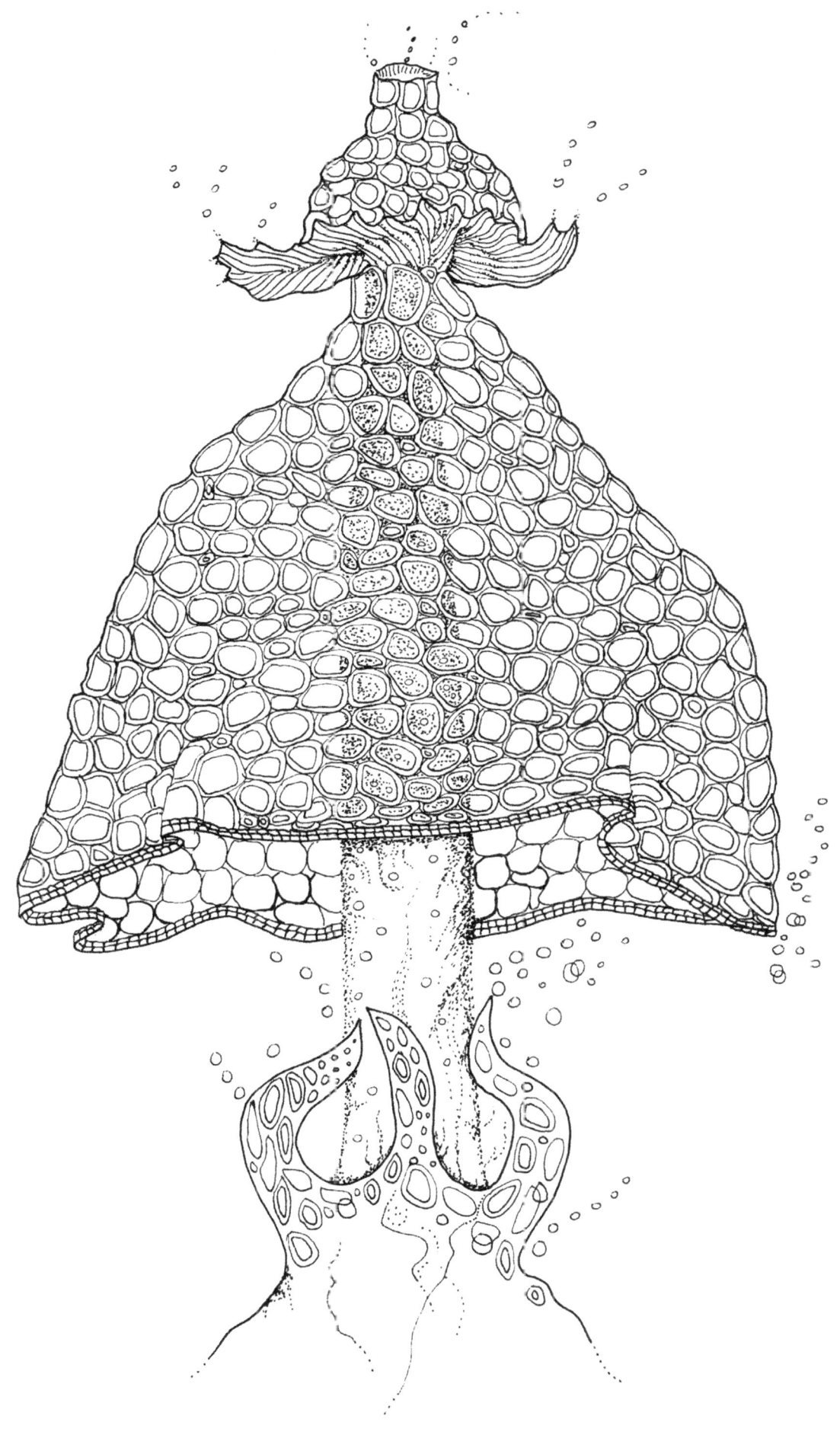

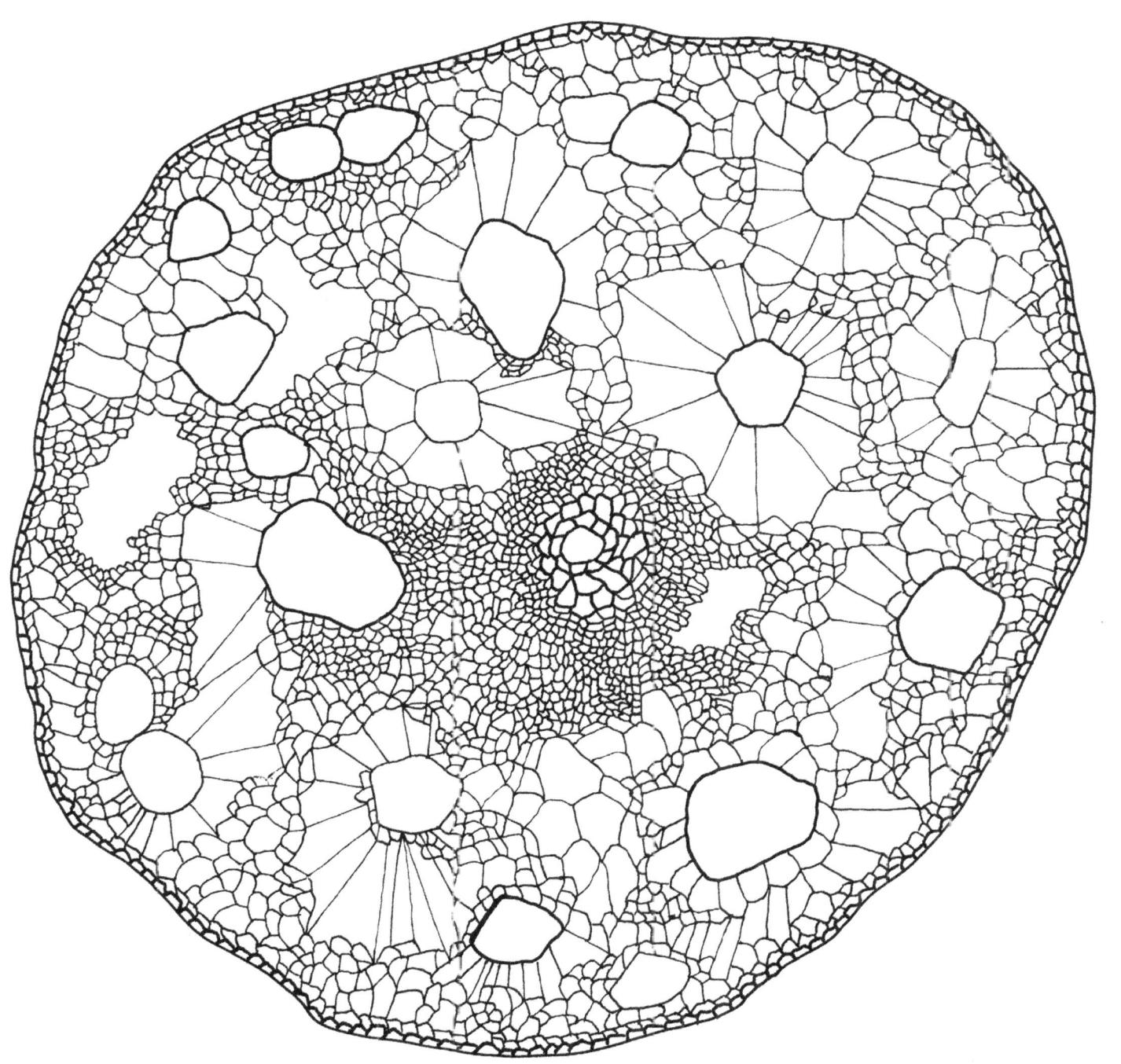

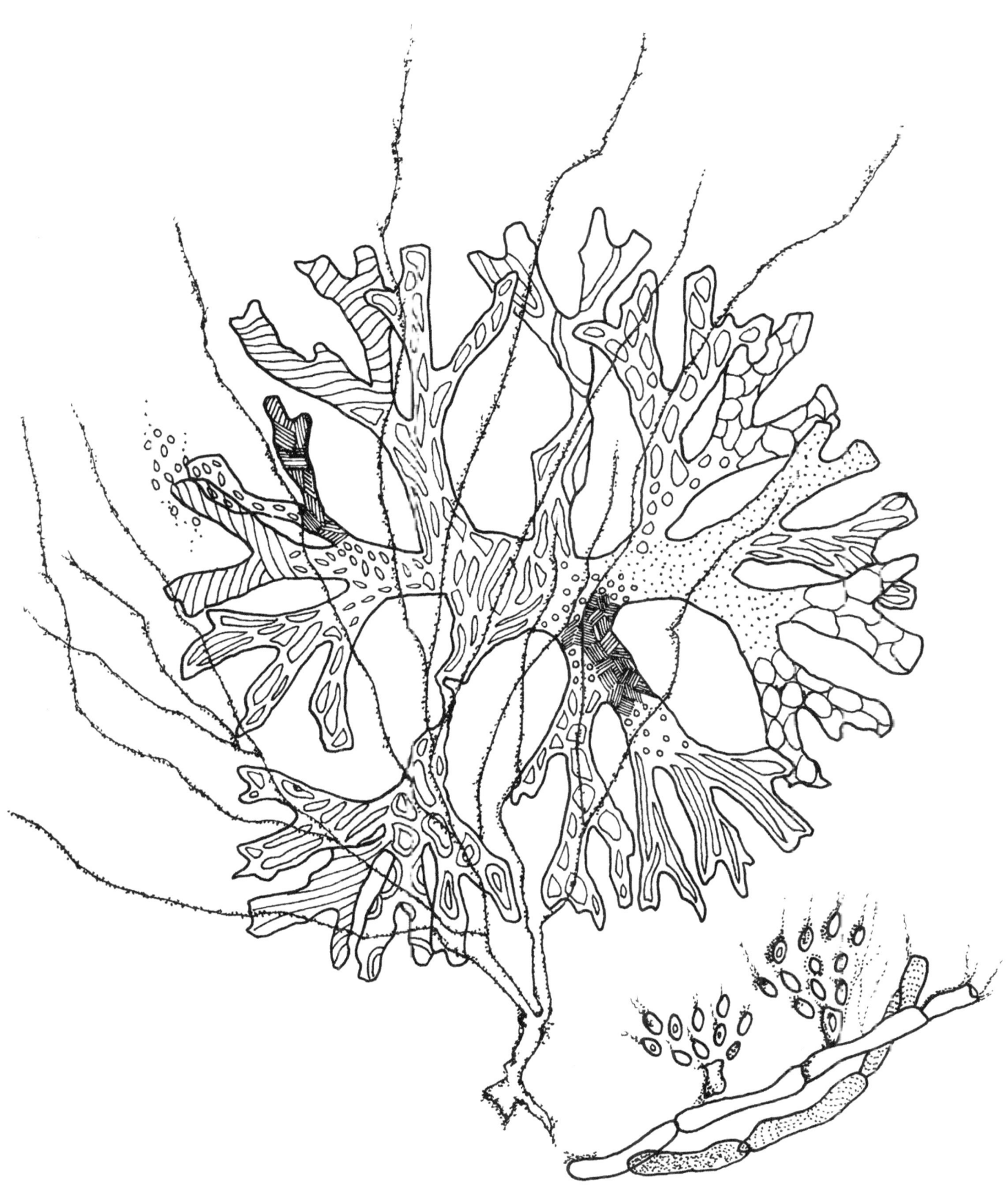

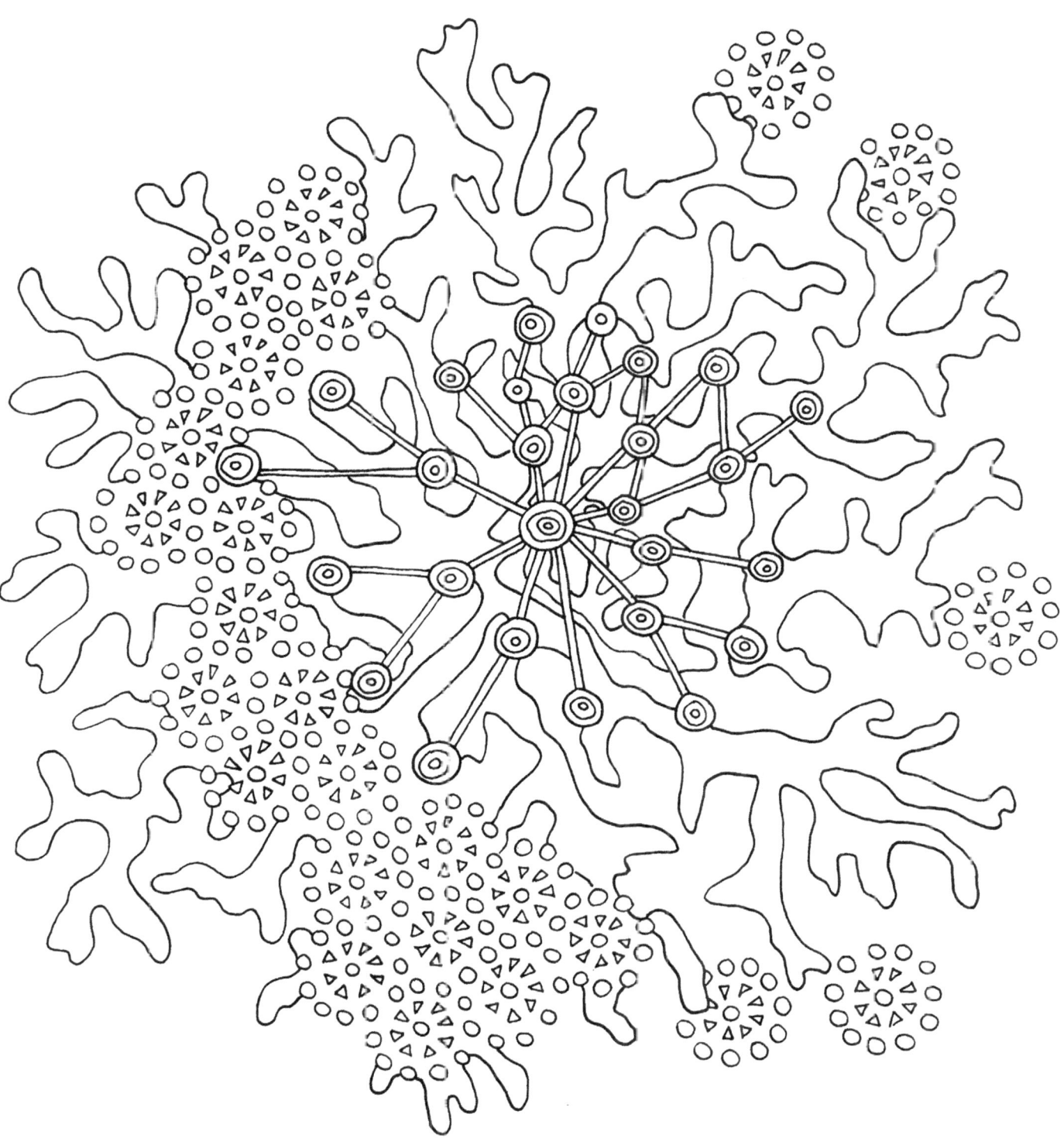

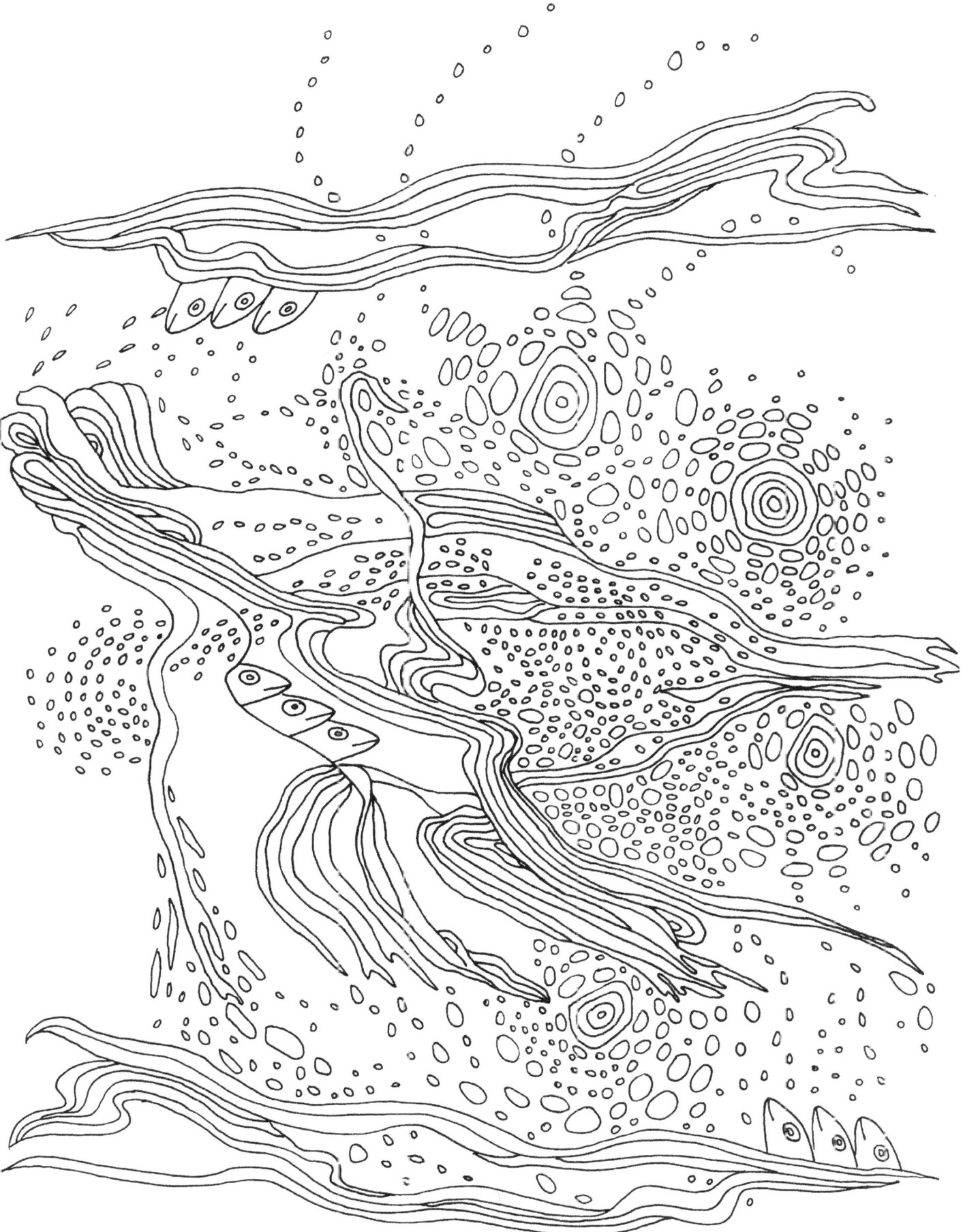

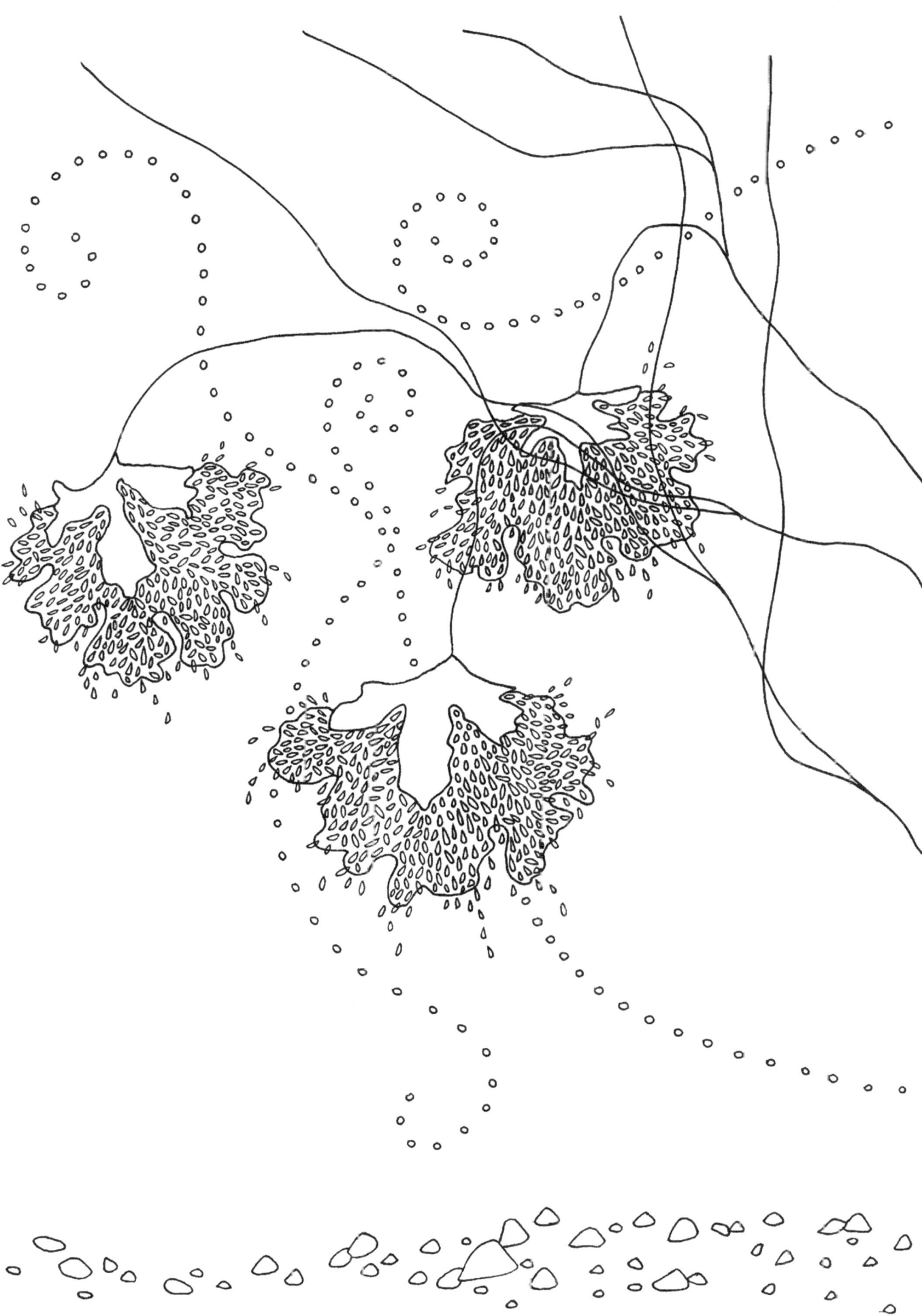

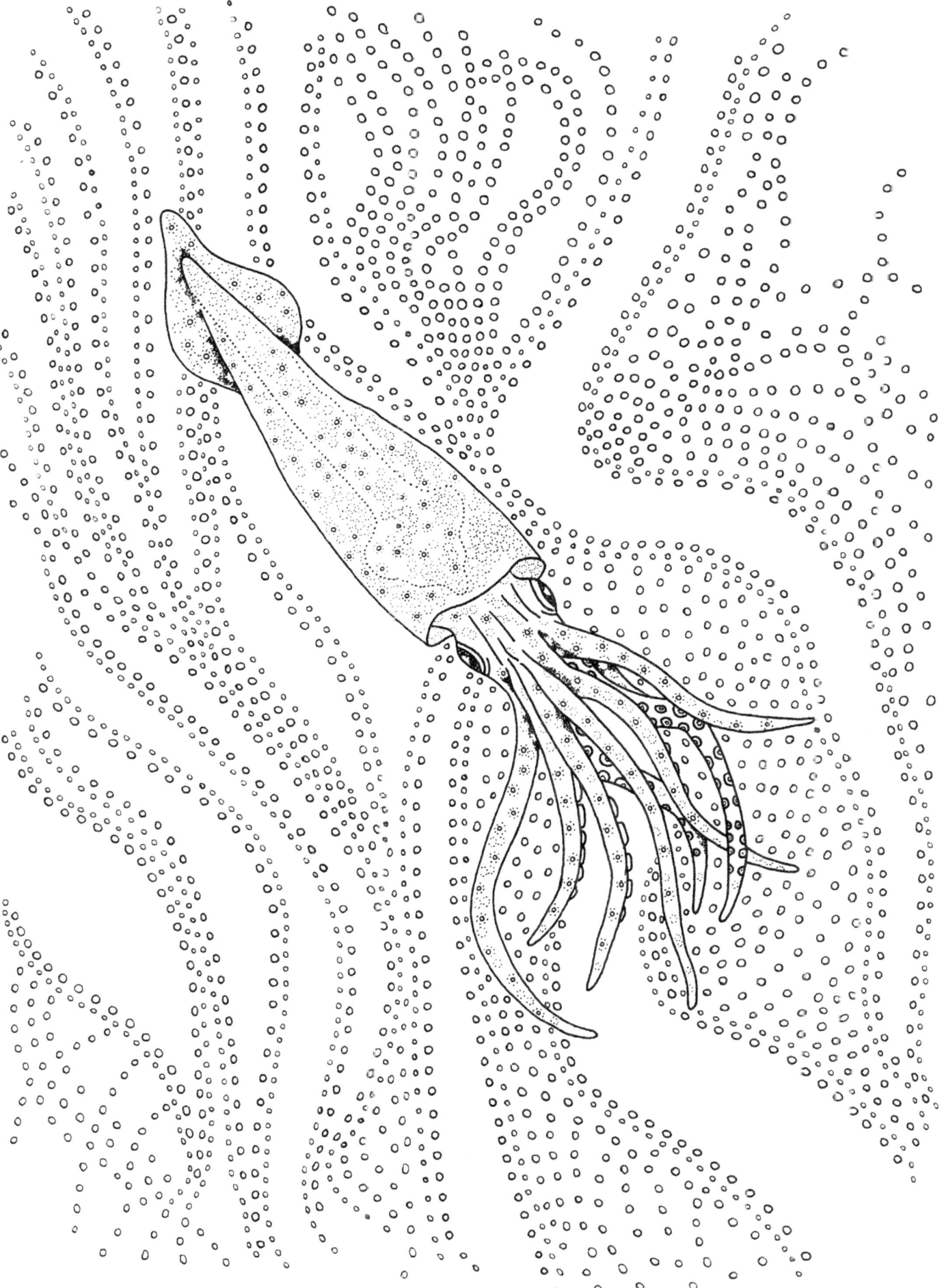

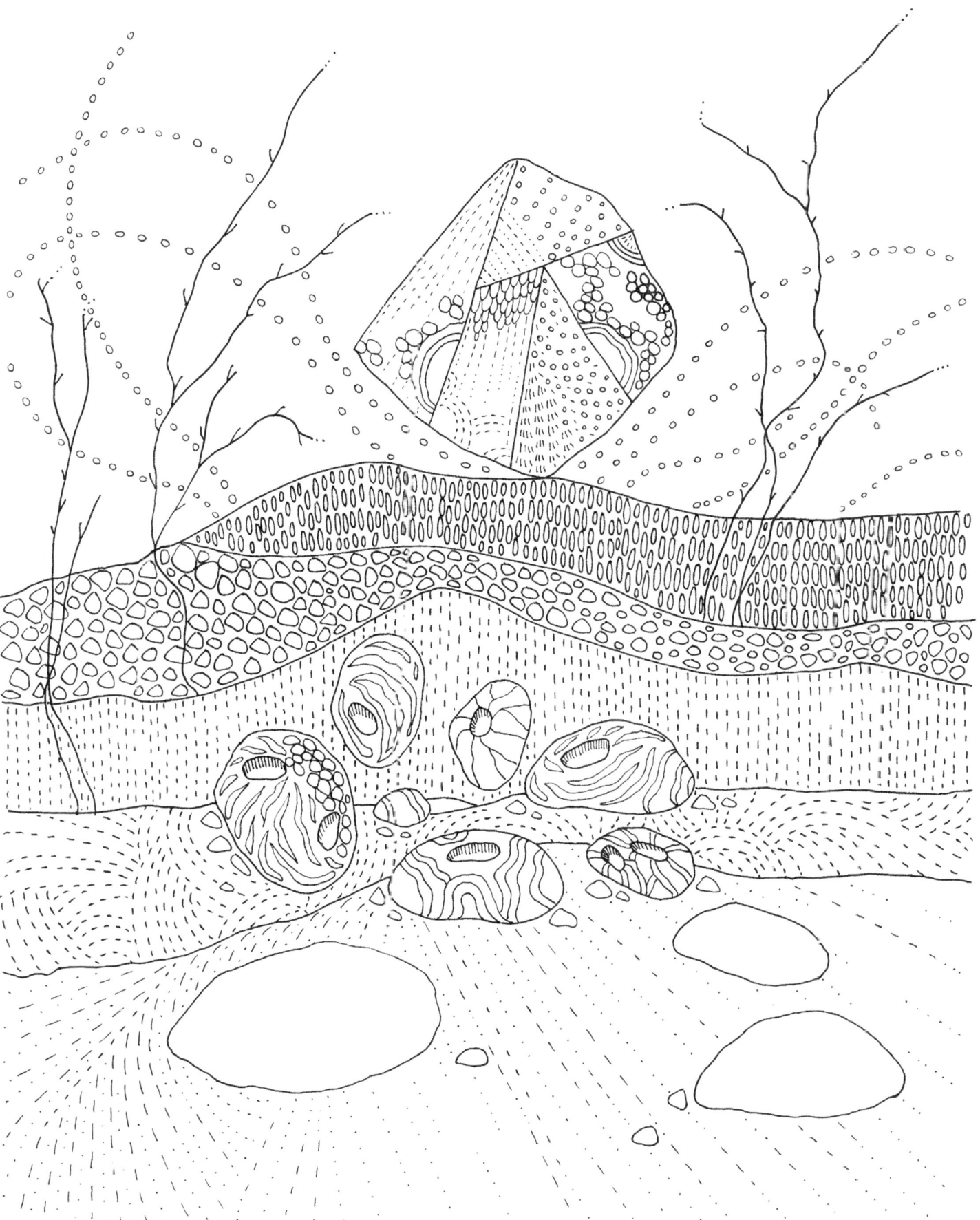

www.ingramcontent.com/pod-product-compliance
Lightning Source LLC
Chambersburg PA
CBHW081553280526
45788CB00011B/3464